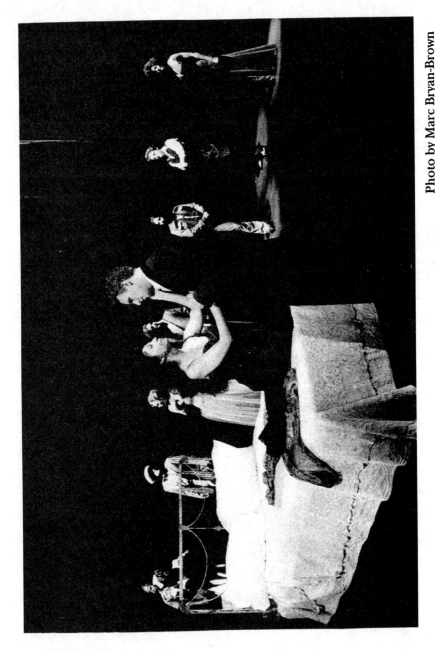

Photo by Marc Bryan-Brown

A scene from the Lincoln Center Theater production of "Hello Again." Set design by Derek McLane.

HELLO AGAIN

A Musical

Words and Music by

MICHAEL JOHN LaCHIUSA

Suggested by the play LA RONDE

by Arthur Schnitzler

★

★

DRAMATISTS
PLAY SERVICE
INC.

HELLO AGAIN was produced at Lincoln Center Theater (André Bishop, Artistic Director; Bernard Gersten, Executive Producer) at the Mitzi E. Newhouse Theater, in New York City, on December 28, 1993. It was directed and the choreography was by Graciela Daniele; the set design was by Derek McLane; the costume design was by Toni-Leslie James; the lighting design was by Jules Fisher and Peggy Eisenhauer; the sound design was by Scott Stauffer; the orchestrations were by Michael Starobin. The cast was as follows:

THE WHORE .... Donna Murphy

THE SOLDIER .... David A. White

THE NURSE.. Judy Blazer

THE COLLEGE BOY .... Michael Park

THE YOUNG WIFE .... Carolee Carmello

THE HUSBAND .... Dennis Parlato

THE YOUNG THING ....John Cameron Mitchell

THE WRITER.. Malcolm Gets

THE ACTRESS .... Michele Pawk

THE SENATOR ....John Dossett

CAST

THE WHORE
THE SOLDIER
THE NURSE
THE COLLEGE BOY
THE YOUNG WIFE
THE HUSBAND
THE YOUNG THING
THE WRITER
THE ACTRESS
THE SENATOR

Scene 1
The Whore and The Soldier — ca. 1900
Scene 2
The Soldier and The Nurse — 1940s
Scene 3
The Nurse and The College Boy — 1960s
Scene 4
The College Boy and The Young Wife — 1930s
Scene 5
The Young Wife and The Husband — 1950s
Scene 6
The Husband and The Young Thing — 1910s
Scene 7
The Young Thing and The Writer — 1970s
Scene 8
The Writer and The Actress — 1920s
Scene 9
The Actress and The Senator — 1980s
Scene 10
The Senator and The Whore — The Present and The Past

AUTHOR'S NOTE

HELLO AGAIN can be thought of as a ballet with words. As conceived by Graciela Daniele, who directed the New York production at Lincoln Center Theater. Its staging and choreography imbue each scene with an important layer of subtext which compliments and sometimes contrasts with the musical subtext and dialogue. Which characters play secondary roles (i.e., the Ship's Steward in Scene 6, or the Swing Quintet in Scene 3) is an important consideration, intrinsic to the score and its vocal arrangements, as well as the psychology of the ballet. For instance, the Whore's appearance in Scene 1, Scene 5 (as the Young Wife's reflection in the mirror), and Scene 10 has a stronger and more mysterious impact, visually and subtextually, then if she were to appear in other scenes.

The following is a breakdown of the secondary roles and what characters play them:

Scene 1: An inebriated MAN: The Senator
Scene 2: SWING TRIO: The Young Wife, The Young Thing, The Actress
SWING QUINTET: The Young Wife, The Young Thing, The Actress, The Husband, The Writer
Scene 3: T.V. REPORTER: The Senator
Scene 4: PATRONS: The Soldier, The Husband, The Young Thing, The Senator
FRED and GINGER: The Writer, The Actress
Scene 5: POP SINGER: The Young Thing
PRIMA DONNA: The Actress
Scene 6: PRIMA DONNA: The Actress
SHIP'S STEWARD: The Senator
PASSENGERS/DISCO REVELERS: Company, except for The Whore
Scene 9: MUSIC VIDEOS: The Soldier, The Nurse
COMPANY: all except The Whore

Michael John La Chiusa

5

HELLO AGAIN

SCENE 1

New York City. The turn of the century. A lamp post near the Hudson River Piers. Twilight.

The Soldier enters. From the shadows, someone calls to him.

WHORE.
 You. You …
(The Soldier stops.)
 HEY.
 THERE.
 WHERE YOU GOIN', SOLDIER?

SOLDIER.
 …? Who me?

WHORE.
 LOOK.
 HERE:
 DON'T YA KNOW MY FACE?

SOLDIER.   *(Peering into the dark.)*
 … No.

WHORE.
 YOU.
 THERE.
 COME 'N TELL YOUR SWEETHEART
 WHERE YOU BEEN —

HEY, IT DON'T MATTER.
HELLO AGAIN ...

SOLDIER.
NO THANKS.
I GOT NO TIME.
AND I GOTTA GET BACK TO THE BARRACKS.

WHORE.
YOU
COULD
JOIN ME BY THE RIVER.

SOLDIER.
DON'T YA GOT A ROOM SOMEWHERE?

WHORE.
TRUST ME.
IT'S THE PERFECT PLACE.

SOLDIER
SMELLS LIKE A SEWER HERE.

WHORE
I BEEN
SEARCHING HIGH AND LOW FOR YOU
BUT THEN —
WHAT DOES IT MATTER?
HELLO AGAIN.

SOLDIER.
I SAID I GOT NO TIME.
AND I GOT NO CASH.
CAN'T PAY FOR IT ANYHOW.

WHORE:
WHO MENTIONED MONEY?
WHO MENTIONED PAY?

GUYS I LIKE DON'T HAVE TO PAY.
GUYS LIKE YOU THEY GET IT FREE.
HERE, BY THE RIVER
EVERYTHING IS FREE ...

SOLDIER.

I HEARD ABOUT YOU AT THE CAFE.
YOU'RE THE ONE WHO GIVES IT AWAY.
YOU GIVE IT AWAY, DON'T YOU?

WHORE.

I WISH
YOU COULD BE MY BOYFRIEND.

SOLDIER.

HA! I'D MAKE YOU JEALOUS!

WHORE.

HUSH.
LOVE.
THE COPS'LL GIVE A CHASE.

SOLDIER.

WHAT COPS?

WHORE.

YOU DON'T HAVE TO REMEMBER
A FACE, A PLACE OR WHEN;
WE MAY DIE TOMORROW.

SOLDIER.

I AIN'T GONNA DIE.

WHORE.

FOR NOW, WATCH YOUR STEP, LOVE;
OR WE'LL DROWN IN THE HUDSON.
HELLO ...

SOLDIER.

    HELLO ....

WHORE.

    HELLO ...

SOLDIER.

    AH HELL ...

(The Whore leads the Soldier into, around, down, through the shadows. She hoists up her skirts. He fucks her, impaling her against the lamppost. Together, they sink to the ground, exhausted.)

WHORE.

    What's your name?

SOLDIER.   *(With a laugh.)*

    My name? Jesus ...

WHORE:

    Hmmm ... mine's Leocadia.

SOLDIER.

    That's a good one.

(He gets up to leave.)

WHORE.

    HEY.

    THERE.

    WHERE YOU GOIN', SOLDIER?

SOLDIER.

    YOU GETTIN' UP?

WHORE.

    COME,

    CLOSE.

    LET ME SEE YOUR FACE.

SOLDIER.

> WHAT FOR?

WHORE.

> YOU DON'T HAVE TO REMEMBER
> A FACE, A PLACE, OR WHEN:
> SO HOW 'BOUT A DIME, LOVE?
> IT'S FOR MY ... DOORMAN.
> WE MAY NEVER BE SAYIN'
> HELLO AGAIN ...

SOLDIER.

> Go to hell. *(He exits.)*

WHORE.

> Hey.... You son of a bitch.

(She notices something missing from her bodice.)

> Hey — where's my brooch? You son of a bitch! You stole my brooch!

Hey!!

(A well-heeled Man [The Senator] stumbles on, drunk. The Whore calls from the shadows.)

> You. You ...

(The Man stops for a moment, then staggers off. The Whore follows.)

SCENE 2

Outside an uptown canteen, 1940s. A Trio (The Actress, The Young Wife, The Young Thing) sings a song of war-time best wishes.

TRIO.

> ZEI GEZENT: BE WELL AND HAPPY.
> ZEI GEZENT: STAY OUT OF TROUBLE'S WAY.
> I'LL TELL YOU WHAT YOU LONG TO HEAR
> WHEN YOUR SHIP SAILS HOME SOMEDAY;
> BUT TILL THEN I'LL SAY:
> Z-ZEI, Z-ZEI, Z-ZEI GEZENT ...

(The Soldier and the Nurse dance on.)

11

NURSE.

Hey.... Where you takin' me?

SOLDIER.

TO HEAVEN.

NURSE.

They don't let types like you in.

SOLDIER.

I'M SHIPPIN' OUT TOMORROW.
DON'T YOU WANNA GIVE A LONELY SOLDIER
SOMETHING
TO REMEMBER YOU BY?

NURSE.

ASK THAT REDHEAD IN THERE.
THE ONE WITH THE FACE.
I seen you dancing her around.

SOLDIER.

You seen everything, huh?

NURSE.

Sure. We nurses see alot.

SOLDIER.   (Grabbing his crotch.)
Help Nurse! I'm wounded!

NURSE.

— Not so fast! I got professional ethics, you know ...

SOLDIER.

I BEEN LOOKIN' FOR YOU
MY WHOLE LIFE ...

NURSE.

Me?

SOLDIER.

I

GOT A LITTLE TIME.

I

I GOT A LITTLE ITCH.

I GOTTA GET THE LITTLE ITCH

SCRATCHED.

AN' WHO'S GONNA HELP ME OUT?

I GOTTA MAKE IT FAST.

THE TIME I GOTTA SCRATCH MY ITCH

MAY BE MY LAST.

I

GOT A LITTLE WAR.

MY

BOAT'S ABOUT TO LEAVE.

WHY

WONDER WHAT WE GONNA DO

WHEN

I GOT A WAD OF DOUGH

AN' THE BEER IS ALL A DIME.

BABY WANT SOME CHICKEN WINGS?

I GOT A LITTLE TIME.

I GOT A LITTLE TIME.

I GOT A LITTLE — GOT A LITTLE — GOT A LITTLE

MY DADDY DON'T CARE WHERE I MAY BE.

MY BROTHER WON'T COME TO LOOK FOR ME.

MY MOMMA DON'T KNOW WHAT SHE DON'T SEE

HEY—

IN PARIS, IT'S THE MORNING.

IN BERLIN, IT'S ALMOST NOON.

IN TOKYO, THE JAPS ARE SMILIN'

AT TOMORROW'S MOON.

IN JUST A LITTLE WHILE

THE WORLD IS GONNA TURN

AND WE GOT JUST A LITTLE TIME

TO HOP AND SHAKE AND BURN —

LET'S BURN!

(A few fascinating steps — he's hot.)

I

GOT A LITTLE TIME.

I

WANNA BE WITH YOU.

I

GOTTA HAVE A LITTLE FUN

NOW.

IN PARIS, IT'S THE MORNING.

IN BERLIN, IT'S ALMOST NOON.

IN TOKYO, THE JAPS ARE SMILIN'

AT TOMORROW'S MOON —

NURSE.

 Hey, Sammy ... baby. Look at the moon ...

(The moon is blinding.)

SOLDIER. *(Collecting himself.)*

 Yeah ...

 I

 GOT A LITTLE TIME.

NURSE.

 YOU

 GOT A

 LITTLE TIME.

BOTH

 WE ...

(A Swing Band Quintet [The Actress, The Young Wife, The Young Thing, The Husband, The Writer] plays. They sway to the music. The Soldier undresses the Nurse. She's tentative. He strokes her breasts. He takes her hands and — she pulls away.)

SOLDIER.

 JESUS CHRIST ALMIGHTY.

NURSE.

 YOU COULD'VE HAD THAT REDHEAD IN THERE.

SOLDIER.
    YEAH.
    SO WHAT?

NURSE.
    SHE'LL SPEND ALL YOUR DOUGH.

SOLDIER.
(And this one's making him pay, too.)
    YEAH, I KNOW.

NURSE.
    YOU THINK I'M PRETTY?

SOLDIER.
    YEAH.

NURSE.
    YOU REALLY THINK I'M PRETTY?

SOLDIER.
    I DON'T WANNA THINK.

NURSE.
    I'M NOT SURE ...

SOLDIER.
    COME ON —

NURSE.
    I THINK —

SOLDIER.
    COME ON, COME ON, COME ON ...
(The Swing Band croons. The Soldier and the Nurse wrestle. This is more work than he bargained for. She's a virgin, not quite sure what to do with her body.)

QUINTET.
> WE KISS
> AND THE ANGELS SIGH.
> WE KISS
> AND OUR TROUBLES FLY.
> THERE ARE SO MANY NEW-FANGLED WAYS
> OF MAKING LOVE
> THAT WE CAN TRY;
> OR WE CAN KISS
> AND THEN SAY
> GOODBYE ...

(Clouds have moved in, erasing the moon. Thunder rolls far away, approaching.)

NURSE.
> Y'GONNA WRITE ME FROM PARIS, AREN'T YA?

SOLDIER.
> YEAH! YEAH ...

NURSE. *(Pulling away.)*
> HEY ...
> CAN'T YOU LEAST SAY THAT YOU LIKE ME?

SOLDIER.
> I TOLD YOU I LIKED YOU.
> PLEASE DON'T TALK.

NURSE.
> HEY ...
> SAY YOU LOVE ME, SAMMY.

SOLDIER. *(Forking it over.)*
> I LOVE YOU.
> STOP CALLING ME SAMMY.
> MY NAME ISN'T SAMMY.

NURSE.
> YOU SAID YOU WERE SAMMY.

SOLDIER.

    MY NAME IS ... LESLIE.

NURSE.

    I THINK ...

SOLDIER.

    DON'T THINK —

NURSE.

    I WANT — I WANT — I WANT —

(She gives in. He turns her over. Lightning flashes; a roll of thunder. A cool rain falls. The Quintet sings.)

QUINTET.

    WE KISS

    AND THE HEAVENS CRY.

    WE KISS

    AND THE ANGELS DIE.

    AFTER TRYING THE ONE OR TWO WAYS

    OF MAKING LOVE

    WE START TO LIE;

(The Soldier comes.)

    BETTER TO KISS

    AND THEN SAY ....

(The Soldier is up and buttoning his uniform. After all this work, was it worth it?)

NURSE.

    HEY ...

    YOU GONNA WALK ME HOME?

SOLDIER.

    SURE.

    RIGHT NOW?

NURSE.

    YEAH.

SOLDIER.

    I NEED A BEER.

NURSE.

    STAY WITH ME.

SOLDIER.

    YOU'RE GONNA GET SOAKED.

NURSE.

    YOU'RE GONNA MAKE FOR THAT REDHEAD —

SOLDIER.

    — AND WHAT IF I DO?
    LOOK: I'M REALLY POOPED.
    AN' I GOTTA LEAVE TOMORROW
    AN' FIGHT A WAR. SO I NEED A BEER.

NURSE.

    I'LL WAIT.

SOLDIER.

    FINE THEN.
    IF YOU WANNA WAIT OUT HERE IN THE RAIN
    YOU GO AHEAD.
    I'M GOING IN
    I NEED A BEER.

(He exits.)

NURSE.

    I LOVE THE RAIN ...
    I'LL WAIT RIGHT HERE ...
    LESLIE
    ... BABY.

(She waits in the rain.)

SCENE 3

A News Reporter (the Senator) appears on a TV screen.

NEWS REPORTER.

... reporting to you live from the Red Cross Hospital in Saigon where twenty-three casualties have been reported since President Johnson ordered additional troops into South Vietnam last year. A shortage of doctors and nurses has prompted Red Cross officials to declare a state of emergency ...

(The College Boy's bedroom, in his parent's home, on the Upper East Side. 1960s. The College Boy has a sprained ankle, so he claims. It's wrapped in an ace bandage. He's reading a book, watching the news. He's bored. He turns off the TV.)

COLLEGE BOY.

Nurse? Nurse? Marie!

(The Nurse has been waiting for his call. She straightens her uniform and hair before entering his bedroom. Their flirtation has been going on for a week.)

NURSE.

Yes...?

COLLEGE BOY.

Hi.

NURSE.

You need something?

COLLEGE BOY.

Uh.... No.... Yes.... Well.... It's hot in here.

NURSE.

You want the fan on?

COLLEGE BOY.

Yes. No. Hot's okay. Never mind.

NURSE.

You want a pain killer?

COLLEGE BOY.

Is Mother home?

NURSE.

No.

COLLEGE BOY.

My dad?

NURSE.

No.

COLLEGE BOY.

The maid?

NURSE.

Out.

COLLEGE BOY.

Just you and I.

NURSE.

JUST YOU AND ME ...

COLLEGE BOY.

So.

NURSE.

How's the ankle today?

COLLEGE BOY.

Awful. I'll never play tennis again.

NURSE.

It's only a sprained ankle. It should have healed a week ago.

COLLEGE BOY.

I told Mother that I didn't need a nurse — but — you know Mother.
... There's no arguing with her. She's just so — *big*.

NURSE.

WHAT'S IT YOU READIN'?

COLLEGE BOY.

STENDAHL.

NURSE.

WHAT'S IT ABOUT?

COLLEGE BOY.

It's ... fascinating. It's for my Romance in World Literature class. I've just
finished his notes on his visit to Florence — Italy?

NURSE.

Yeah.

COLLEGE BOY.

And, well ... he was touring all these cathedrals and at one particular
cathedral, these frescoes — paintings?

NURSE.

Yeah?

COLLEGE BOY.

These frescoes so overwhelmed him that —
HE THOUGHT HE WAS DYING.

NURSE.

YEAH.

COLLEGE BOY.

KNOW HOW HE CALMED HIMSELF DOWN?

NURSE.

HOW?

21

COLLEGE BOY.

    By ... reading poetry!

NURSE.

    Oh God.

COLLEGE BOY.

    But isn't that fascinating?
    WHAT THAT MUST FEEL LIKE ...

NURSE.

    Reading poems?

COLLEGE BOY.

    Dying ... *(The Nurse sighs, giggles.)*
    I KNOW WHAT I NEED.
    I NEED ...
    Water.

NURSE.

    Okay.

(She exits. He leaps up, combs his hair, dabs cologne. She fluffs up her bosom, straightens her nursing tights. She re-enters with water.)

    Water.

COLLEGE BOY.

    Yum. Do you ... have a boyfriend?

NURSE.

    No.

COLLEGE BOY.

    EVER?

NURSE.

    MAYBE.

COLLEGE BOY.

Do I look like Bobby Kennedy?

NURSE.

Bobby Kennedy? Sure.

COLLEGE BOY.

Why are you looking at me like that?

NURSE.

Like what?

COLLEGE BOY.

Like ...

NURSE.

LIKE I WANNA DO THIS?

(She begins to strip.)

COLLEGE BOY.

I meant — what — huh ...

NURSE.

LIKE I WANNA DO ... THIS?

COLLEGE BOY.

What if Mother...?

NURSE.

YOUR MOMMA DON'T KNOW WHAT SHE DON'T SEE.
RIGHT?

(She starts to slip out of her uniform.)

COLLEGE BOY.

What do you think about U.S. involvement with Southeast Asia?

NURSE.

I SHOULD'VE MET YOU IN SOME OTHER LIFE.

COLLEGE BOY.

    We aren't violating any professional ethics, are we?

NURSE.

    I SHOULD'VE MET YOU IN SOME OTHER TIME.
    WOULD'VE BEEN SWEETER
    KISSING YOU.
    WOULD'VE BEEN BETTER WITH
    SOMEONE SOFTER, SOMEONE EASY,
    SOMEONE YOUNGER, SOMEONE LIKE MYSELF —
    MYSELF – MYSELF – MYSELF – BUT
    OTHER THINGS HAPPENED IN SOME OTHER LIFE.
    IT DON'T MATTER WHAT OR WHEN OR WHO.
    SOME LITTLE BIT OF ME'S GONE.
    I'M GONNA STEAL A LITTLE BIT OF YOU.

COLLEGE BOY.

    You're not a virgin are you?

NURSE.

    Yeah. Be gentle.
(She ties him up with her stockings.)
    BABY, THERE'S A REVOLUTION GOIN' ON
    AND IT'S HARD TO KEEP MY COOL.
    THERE'S SOME THINGS THEY DIDN'T TEACH ME
    BACK IN NURSING SCHOOL.
    LIKE HOW MEN ARE GONNA TAKE AN' TAKE AN' TAKE
    AN' TAKE AN' NOT GIVE NOTHIN' BACK;
    A SOLDIER I KNEW;
    THEN THAT RED-HEADED TEEN;
    THE GUY IN THE PARK
    BY THE PEPSI MACHINE.
    THE FIRST TIME AN' LAST TIME
    AN' TIME IN-BETWEEN —
    I SHOULD'VE LOVED YOU IN SOME OTHER LIFE,
    NOW I ALWAYS FEEL LIKE I'M AT WAR.
    SOMEBODY TOOK WHAT WAS MINE,
    I SAY THAT AIN'T GONNA DO.

I WANT A LITTLE BIT, GIVE ME A LITTLE BIT,
I'M GONNA STEAL A LITTLE BIT OF YOU —

(She has an orgasm — and another.)

YOU ... YOU ... YOU ... YOU ...

(And then: nothing.)

YOU.

COLLEGE BOY.

My ankle feels better.

NURSE.

Good.... Pass the water.

COLLEGE BOY.   *(His hands still tied, he passes her the water.)*

I ought to get my own apartment.... Love is a terribly confusing ordeal, isn't it?

NURSE.   *(Drinking.)*

Mmmm ...

COLLEGE BOY.   *(He starts – a noise downstairs.)*

... Who's home!? Mother? Is that you?...

NO ONE....

I MIGHT NOT BE NEEDING A NURSE.

SOON.

NURSE.

OH?

COLLEGE BOY.

Well. We'll see what Mother says. She pays for your services. Not I. Untie me?

NURSE.

My shift's over.

(She gathers up her uniform and takes his book. She exits.)

COLLEGE BOY.
 Hey...? Marie? Nurse...?
(He tries to chew through her stocking ...)
 Nurse!

SCENE 4

Movie house, 1930s. A movie is in progress: a Hollywood musical. A few pa-trons are slumped in their seats. [The Young Thing, The Husband, The Sena-tor, The Soldier]

Young Wife is seated. She wears a hat with a heavy veil.

College Boy enters, looking for her.

COLLEGE BOY.
 Is that you?

YOUNG WIFE.
 Who is that?

COLLEGE BOY.
 Me!

YOUNG WIFE.
 Where have you been!?

COLLEGE BOY.
 Take off the hat.

YOUNG WIFE.
 What if —

COLLEGE BOY.
>   Here —

YOUNG WIFE.
>   No !

COLLEGE BOY.
>   How is it pinned —?

YOUNG WIFE.
>   OUCH!

COLLEGE BOY.
>   OUCH!

BOTH.
>   OUCH!

PATRONS.
>   SHHH!

(A pause.)

YOUNG WIFE.
>   I've been waiting for hours!

COLLEGE BOY.
>   I had to stay after class —

YOUNG WIFE.
>   It's an awful movie.

COLLEGE BOY.
>   Forgive me.

YOUNG WIFE.
>   Fred Astaire dancing on a boat.

COLLEGE BOY.
>   I missed you.

YOUNG WIFE.

    This is wrong. What if someone finds out!?

COLLEGE BOY.

    Who?

YOUNG WIFE.

    My husband!

COLLEGE BOY.

    Him. You're too young for him.

YOUNG WIFE.

    You're too young for me. I'm leaving.

COLLEGE BOY.

    No!

    I SHOULD HAVE FOUND YOU IN SOME OTHER LIFE.

    I SHOULD HAVE FOUND YOU BEFORE YOU WERE MARRIED ...

YOUNG WIFE.

    If my husband finds out he'll throw me out on the street and I'll have
to sell pencils or ... apples ... or other things ...

(They kiss. They watch the movie.)

COLLEGE BOY.

    REMEMBER LAST TIME —

YOUNG WIFE.

    IN THE PARK.

COLLEGE BOY.

    IN THAT ROWBOAT.

YOUNG WIFE.

    WE WERE NAKED —

COLLEGE BOY.
　　IT WAS PERFECT —

YOUNG WIFE.
　　IT WAS COLD.
　　... WHAT IF MY HUSBAND—?

COLLEGE BOY.
　　HE'S A BORE —

YOUNG WIFE.
　　HE SUPPORTS ME —

COLLEGE BOY.
　　AND HE'S STUFFY —

YOUNG WIFE.
　　HE'S IN BUSINESS —

COLLEGE BOY.
　　AND HE'S OLD.

YOUNG WIFE.
　　I'm leaving.

COLLEGE BOY.
　　No!

YOUNG WIFE.
　　I'M MORALLY BANKRUPT.
　　MY REPUTATION IS AT STAKE!
　　MY MARRIAGE IS AT STAKE!
　　HE GIVES ME EVERYTHING!
　　WELL.
　　ALMOST EVERYTHING.
　　I HATE TO LIE TO HIM.
　　HE'S GOING OUT OF TOWN NEXT WEEK —

COLLEGE BOY.
    THAT'S GOOD.

YOUNG WIFE.
    — AGAIN.

COLLEGE BOY.
    YOU HAVE TO LEAVE HIM —

YOUNG WIFE.
    YOU'RE INSANE —

COLLEGE BOY.
    BUT I LOVE YOU —

YOUNG WIFE.
    PLEASE DON'T LOVE ME —

COLLEGE BOY.
    BUT I LOVE YOU

YOUNG WIFE.
    THIS IS WRONG.

PATRON.
    Shhh!

YOUNG WIFE.
    At Miss Farmingham's I was voted "Most likely to Succeed." Ha!
    I'M MORALLY BANKRUPT!
    I HATE GINGER ROGERS.
    I THINK THAT I'M DYING!
(She gets on her knees before him, and tries to arouse him.)

PATRON.
    I HAVE TO —
    RELAX AND —
    JUST LET HER —

COLLEGE BOY.
     SWEET JESUS —

PATRONS.
     ENJOY IT —

PATRONS/COLLEGE BOY.
     STAY FOCUSED —

PATRONS.
     HER TONGUE IS —

COLLEGE BOY.
     HER LIPS ARE —

PATRONS/COLLEGE BOY.
     I KNOW THERE'S TROUBLE AHEAD.

COLLEGE BOY.
     WHY CAN'T I GET IT UP
     AND KEEP IT UP
     WITHOUT ALL THE WORK?
     THE STORY OF MY LIFE.
     IT'S JUST THE SORRY LITTLE STORY
     OF MY LIFE.

PATRON.
     IMPOTENCE:

COLLEGE BOY.
     I'D NEVER DREAMED IT WOULD OCCUR;
     THAT IS, TILL I MET HER:
     THE ONE I THINK I LOVE.

PATRONS.
     LET'S FACE THE MUSIC INSTEAD.

COLLEGE BOY.

       I'VE NEVER WORKED SO HARD

       TO KEEP IT HARD —

       AND THEN I MET HER.

       AND HAD HER.

       AND THEN I

       LOST INTEREST.

PATRONS.

       IT'S HER FAULT.

COLLEGE BOY.

       IT'S MY FAULT

       TO THINK THAT STEALING SOMEONE'S

       LONELY LITTLE WIFE

       WOULD BE THE GREATEST OF ADVENTURES

       OF THE SORRY LITTLE

       STORY OF MY LIFE ...

(He's gone limp. She pokes her head up and climbs back into her seat. Her lipstick is smeared. She fixes it.)

YOUNG WIFE.

       WE'VE GOT A PROBLEM.

       ONCE AGAIN.

COLLEGE BOY.

       WHAT DOES *THAT* MEAN?

YOUNG WIFE.

       IT'S A PROBLEM.

COLLEGE BOY.

       I CAN'T HELP IT.

YOUNG WIFE.

       NO YOU CAN'T ...

       IT HAPPENED LAST TIME.

COLLEGE BOY.
        WHEN WAS THAT?

YOUNG WIFE.
        IN THE ROWBOAT.

COLLEGE BOY.
        I WAS FREEZING.

YOUNG WIFE.
        IS IT MY FAULT?

COLLEGE BOY.
        TRY AGAIN.

YOUNG WIFE.
        No!

COLLEGE BOY.
        You were voted Most Likely to Succeed.

YOUNG WIFE.
        The floor is filthy! Look: Popcorn on my knees.

COLLEGE BOY.
        THEY SAY ...
        WHEN A MAN IS WITH THE ONE HE TRULY LOVES ...
        Sometimes ... he can't ... they say.

YOUNG WIFE.
        Who says?

COLLEGE BOY.
        Stendhal.
        IT'S A STORY —
        A SOLDIER
        WHEN HE'S WITH THE ONE HE LOVES —
        HE CAN'T —

YOUNG WIFE.

Oh.

COLLEGE BOY.

AND HE CRIES.

YOUNG WIFE.

You're not going to cry, are you?

COLLEGE BOY.

You want me to fail.
LIKE MY FATHER.
LIKE MY MOTHER.
EVERYBODY.

YOUNG WIFE.

You didn't tell your Stendhal friend about us, did you?

COLLEGE BOY.

Maybe your husband should know about us.

YOUNG WIFE.

I'm leaving.

COLLEGE BOY.

Fine, go.

YOUNG WIFE.

I'M NOT YOUR FATHER.
I'M NOT YOUR MOTHER.
I'M NOT YOUR MAID OR YOUR NURSE.
I'M A MARRIED WOMAN.

(She disappears below the seats. The screen flickers. Fred and Ginger [The Writer and The Actress] dance ecstatically.)

PATRONS.

I HAVE TO —
JUST THINK OF —
BEFORE SHE —

GAVE INTO —
BEFORE I —
COULD HAVE HER —
MOST LIKELY —
SUCCEEDING —
AH!

(He comes. She climbs back into her seat.)

YOUNG WIFE.

That was quick ...
LOOK AT MY KNEECAPS.
AND MY DRESS.
IT'S DISGUSTING.
IT'S UNHEALTHY.
THIS IS SICKNESS ...
I need *more* ...

COLLEGE BOY.

I don't. I have everything now.

YOUNG WIFE.

When can I see you again?

COLLEGE BOY.

YOU HAVE A HUSBAND.

YOUNG WIFE.

I DON'T CARE.
I HAVE TO SEE YOU.

COLLEGE BOY.

WELL —

YOUNG WIFE.

SOMEPLACE —

COLLEGE BOY.

WELL —
THE ZOO?

YOUNG WIFE.

    The zoo!

    I'M MORALLY BANKRUPT!

    HAVE I REDUCED MYSELF TO THIS!

    THIS CHEAP AND SICK AFFAIR.

    I WAS AN INNOCENT.

    WELL ... ALMOST INNOCENT.

    IN FRONT OF ANIMALS!

    THE ZOO!

    When?

COLLEGE BOY.

    Soon.

YOUNG WIFE.

    Tomorrow!

COLLEGE BOY.

    I've got an American History class. I'll call you —

YOUNG WIFE.

    No! Tomorrow.

COLLEGE BOY.

    Tomorrow. I have to leave, darling. Mother is expecting me for dinner.
I'll go first. I love you.

(He rises.)

    Now it won't go down.

YOUNG WIFE.

    I'M MORALLY BANKRUPT.

PATRONS.

    SHH!

(She smiles and enjoys the movie.)

SCENE 5

A radio plays, early 50s rock-n-roll. A young Neil Sedaka-type Pop Singer [The Young Thing] performs.

POP SINGER.
> DONNA LOVES BOBBY
> AND BOBBY LOVES SUE.
> SUE LOVES JIMMY
> AND JIMMY LOVES YOU
> YOU LOVE RONNY
> AND I LOVE HIM TOO;
> BUT IT'S THE PROM
> AND I AIN'T GONNA CRY.
> I AIN'T GONNA CRY,
> I AIN'T GONNA CRY —

(The bedroom of an upper-middle-class couple; a bed, a vanity, a dressing mirror. 1950s. The Husband enters in a tuxedo.)

HUSBAND.
> Are you ready? Poodle?

POP SINGER.
> — NOT AT THE PROM
> I'LL DANCE WITH SOMEBODY ELSE
> I'LL DANCE WITH SOMEBODY —

(The Husband switches stations; something operatic. A Prima Donna [The Actress] performs.)

PRIMA DONNA.
> AH, MAIEN ZEIT!
> ADE NUN, HELLES LUSTGETON!
> AH, MAIEN ZEIT!
> ADE DU JUNGES LIEBEN;
> DU WARST SO SCHOEN, SCHOEN;
> DU WARST SO SCHOEN —

(The Wife enters, turns off the radio. She sits at her vanity.)

HUSBAND.

We're going to miss the first act.

YOUNG WIFE.

I know.

HUSBAND.

The best music is in the first act.

YOUNG WIFE.

Can't we stay home tonight? Just watch television.

HUSBAND.

And miss the opera?

YOUNG WIFE.

Uncle Miltie is on.

HUSBAND.

Milton Berle is a cheap clown. Renata Tebaldi is a gift from God. Besides, I have business associates to meet there. I don't see my luggage.

YOUNG WIFE.

Luggage?

HUSBAND.

I'm sailing for London tomorrow. You were going to pack for me.

YOUNG WIFE.

Tomorrow?

HUSBAND.

Silly poodle. We're getting forgetful in our old age.

YOUNG WIFE.

WHAT'S TODAY?

HUSBAND.
> Monday.

YOUNG WIFE.
> No — THE DATE.

HUSBAND.
> The twelfth. May. Of course.

YOUNG WIFE.
> OF COURSE.
> Remember our honeymoon?
> PALM BEACH ... I WISH THAT ... WE ... YOU ...
> Are you tired of me?

HUSBAND.
> Tired of you? Angel ... I don't always show it but I love you absolutely.
> It's just — sometimes I like to forget that I do.

YOUNG WIFE.
> You like to forget.

HUSBAND.
> THE GREATEST OF ADVENTURES
> IS REMEMBERING HOW MUCH
> I LOVE YOU.

YOUNG WIFE.
> What?

HUSBAND.
> IF I LOVED YOU EVERY SECOND,
> EVERY MINUTE, EVERY DAY,
> WE'D BE BORED.

YOUNG WIFE.
> Bored.

HUSBAND.
>FORGETTING NOW AND THEN
>KEEPS A MARRIAGE FULL OF LIFE;
>FORGETTING HELPS TO KEEP
>OUR ROMANCE NEW.

YOUNG WIFE.
>New.

HUSBAND.
>IT'S LIKE A SECOND HONEYMOON
>EVERYTIME THAT I RECALL
>THE ANGEL THAT I FOUND BACK THEN
>IN YOU ...
>I've had at least a thousand honeymoons since our wedding night.

YOUNG WIFE.
>I see ... Marianne is having an affair.

HUSBAND.
>What?

YOUNG WIFE.
>HER LOVER IS A COLLEGE BOY.

HUSBAND.
>Well. I don't think you should associate with this Marianne.
>IT REFLECTS UPON YOUR CHARACTER AND MINE.
>I have a business, remember?

YOUNG WIFE.
>Uh-huh.

HUSBAND.
>YOUR FRIEND WILL HAVE TO PAY
>FOR HER SORDID LITTLE NEED FOR ....

YOUNG WIFE.
  PLEASURE.

HUSBAND.
  Carnal gratification. I don't think you understand what that kind of woman is up to. That kind of woman is morally bankrupt. No better than ... a prostitute.

YOUNG WIFE.
  DO YOU?
  OR, BEFORE WE WERE MARRIED?
  DID YOU?

HUSBAND.
  Did I what?

YOUNG WIFE.
  We've been married five years and I still don't know your past. Did you ever know that kind of woman?

HUSBAND.
  Yes. And it's a sad part of my past. And I would suppose that that young woman is dead now.
  THAT TYPE OF GIRL DIES YOUNG.

YOUNG WIFE.   *(Handing him her shoes.)*
  Why'd you do it?

HUSBAND.
  For ... gratification.

YOUNG WIFE.
  Ah ... carnal gratification.

HUSBAND.
  If I hadn't met you, Angel ... God knows what I would've been like.

YOUNG WIFE.

    God knows.

HUSBAND.

    THE GREATEST OF ADVENTURES
    WHICH A MAN AND WOMAN SHARE
    IS MARRIAGE.
    Repeat ...

YOUNG WIFE.

    THE GREATEST OF ADVENTURES
    WHICH A MAN AND WOMAN SHARE
    IS MARRIAGE.

HUSBAND.

    Good.
    CHEATING ON ONE'S HUSBAND ISN'T WISE.
    MARRIAGE CANNOT TOLERATE LIES.

YOUNG WIFE.

    LIES.

HUSBAND.

    THE GREATEST OF ADVENTURES
    WE HAVE CHOSEN, MY LOVE,
    THERE'S NO TURNING BACK,
    EMILY.
    PLEASE DON'T FORGET?

YOUNG WIFE.

    I WON'T.

HUSBAND.

    THERE'S NO TURNING —
(She suddenly pulls him to her. She takes him down on the bed.)
    But ... the opera ... Emily.... We'll get wrinkled ...

(He acquiesces to her. He makes love to her dutifully. It isn't what she wants after all. She substitutes a pillow for herself and leaves the bed and her Husband. She goes to the dressing mirror and meets her reflection [the Whore]. She fantasizes.)

YOUNG WIFE.
> ONE YEAR AGO.
> THE TWELFTH OF MAY.
> THAT LUNCHEONETTE
> WHERE HE APPEARS
> I SEE HIM FIRST.
> AND THEN HE SMILES
> I WON'T FORGET.
> I WON'T FORGET ...
> SOMETHING SAD IS PLAYING ON THE JUKEBOX;
> A GIRL WHO'S LOST HER BOYFRIEND TO A FRIEND.
> I CAN'T REMEMBER MY HUSBAND'S FACE.
> I CAN'T REMEMBER MY LOVER'S FACE.
> BUT I CAN REMEMBER A STRANGER'S FACE:
> HIS NAME IS TOM.
>
> I LEAVE A TIP.
> DO NOT LOOK BACK.
> I REACH THE PARK.
> AND HE APPEARS.
> THAT BRILLIANT SMILE.
> THOSE TWO-TONED SHOES.
> HIS EYES ARE GREEN.
> HE SAYS HELLO ...
> SUDDENLY THE CITY FEELS ON FIRE.
> IT'S LIKE THE WORLD HAS FIN'LLY
> REACHED AN END.
> I DON'T REMEMBER MY HUSBAND'S VOICE.
> I DON'T REMEMBER MY LOVER'S VOICE.
> BUT I DO REMEMBER I HEAR THAT VOICE
> AND I'M WANTING TO RUN —
> WANTING TO CRY —
> WANTING TO SCREAM —

I —
I ASK HIS NAME —

AND WE KISS
AND THE ANGELS SIGH.
WE KISS
AND THE HEAVENS SMILE.
WE FLY LIKE ANGELS
WOULD LIKE TO FLY;
WE KISS AND SAY ...
GOODBYE ...

(Her fantasy ends. She makes her way back to the bed, removing the pillow, substituting herself under her Husband.)

WHAT'S BETTER IS
WHAT WOULD HAVE BEEN.
WHAT'S SWEETER IS
WHAT WOULD HAVE BEEN.
THE TWELFTH OF MAY.
THAT BRILLIANT SMILE.
THE GREATEST OF ADVENTURES
OF MY LIFE...!

(Her Husband climaxes with her. He rolls away from her.)

HUSBAND.
　　Palm Beach.... What a little angel you were then. Well.... So much for the opera.... Please don't forget to pack my luggage first thing tomorrow morning ... I'll bring you a present from London.

(He rests in her lap.)

YOUNG WIFE.
　　I CAN'T REMEMBER MY HUSBAND'S NAME.
　　I CAN'T REMEMBER MY LOVER'S NAME.
　　BUT I CAN REMEMBER
　　WHAT WOULD HAVE BEEN.
　　IT HAS A NAME ...

(She stares into the dark.)

SCENE 6

An elegantly dressed Prima Donna [The Actress] sings.

PRIMA DONNA.
>AH, MAIEN ZEIT!
>ADE NUN, HELLES LUSTGETON;
>AH, MAIEN ZEIT!
>ADE DU JUNGES LIEBEN;
>DU WARST SO SCHOEN, SO SCHOEN;
>DU WARST SO SCHOEN ...

(A first-class stateroom on a luxury liner, 1912. Late evening. The ship's orchestra plays. The Husband is entertaining a Young Thing. The Young Thing is androgynous.)

YOUNG THING.
>LISTEN TO THAT ORCHESTRA.
>THEY'RE PLAYING AWFUL LATE.
>I FANCY FIRST-CLASS.
>IT'S SO CROWDED IN STEERAGE.
>SIX BUNKS TO A CABIN.
>IMAGINE!
>WITH ALL THE ROOM ON THIS BOAT
>THEY STICK SIX TO A CELL.
>YOU CAN'T IMAGINE THE SMELL
>OF SIX OF US CRAMMED *(Hiccup.)* IN A CABIN.
>... WHAT'S THAT TUNE?

HUSBAND.
>SOME OPERETTA.
>THE CELLO'S FLAT.
>IT'S REALLY QUITE ANNOYING.
>More wine?

YOUNG THING.
>Thank you, sir ... *(Drinking daintily.)* See? I remember what you taught me:

LIFT THE WINE GLASS SLOWLY AS YOU BRING IT TO YOUR LIPS;
DON'T GUZZLE.

HUSBAND.

Perfect.

(A gentle Barcarolle plays.)

YOUNG THING.

THIS IS A SHIP OF DREAMS.

HUSBAND.

You mentioned that your mother sent you away to London — because?

YOUNG THING.

Because ... well .... She didn't think Philadelphia was safe for young
adults.... In London I lived with an uncle. He was real nice to me. But
then ...

HUSBAND.

Yes.

YOUNG THING.

Well.

HIS WIFE DIDN'T LIKE ME.

WHICH FORK DO I USE ON THE SALMON?

HUSBAND.

And you're returning home to your mother?

YOUNG THING.

Not actually.

WHEN I LAND IN NEW YORK

I SUPPOSE I'LL BE OUT ON MY OWN.

SIR.

WHEN I LAND IN NEW YORK

I SUPPOSE I'LL BE LOST AND ALONE.

CARL.

IS YOUR NAME REALLY CARL?

HUSBAND.

    Of course.

YOUNG THING.   *(Opening a tiny gift box.)*

    What's this? A brooch ...

    PRETTY GIFTS FOR A PRETTY WIFE?

    What's her name?

HUSBAND.

    MARIANNE.

YOUNG THING.

    What's her real name?

HUSBAND.

    EMILY ...

    THE GREATEST OF ADVENTURES

    WHICH A MAN AND WOMAN SHARE

    IS MARRIAGE ...

YOUNG THING.

    IT'S YOUR EYES.

    They remind me of my long-lost father.

HUSBAND.

    You said you never knew your father.

YOUNG THING.

    I GOT PICTURES.

HUSBAND.

    When I saw you board at Southampton I thought: there you were, all
    alone.

    SAILING ACROSS THE SEA.

YOUNG THING.

    SWELTERING IN STEERAGE.

HUSBAND.
    LOOKING LOST AND HUNGRY.

YOUNG THING.
    FATHERLESS ...

HUSBAND.
    FATHERLESS ...

YOUNG THING.
    PENNILESS ...

HUSBAND.
    INNOCENT.
    REMINDING ME OF ... ME.

YOUNG THING.
    And you came all the way down to third-class to find me.

HUSBAND.
    I thought: I've always ... but. I've been looking for someone.

YOUNG THING.
    AIN'T WE ALL?
(The orchestra strikes up a jaunty Habanera.)
    What's that tune?
    I GOTTA USE THE POT.
(The Young Thing exits. There's a knock at the door. The Husband answers it. A Ship's Steward [the Senator] enters, life-belts in hand.)

HUSBAND.
    I asked not to be disturbed.

STEWARD.
    I beg your pardon, sir, but the Captain has requested that all passengers don their life jackets and report to their lifeboat stations.

HUSBAND.

What has happened?

STEWARD.

Seems we've struck a bit of ice, sir.

HUSBAND.

Is it serious?

STEWARD.

Women and children are being lowered, sir.

HUSBAND.

Ridiculous, This ship can't — We're sinking?

STEWARD.

Rather quickly.

HUSBAND.

But — what should I do?

STEWARD.

I'd hurry topside, sir.
(*He exits. Husband closes the door. He's stunned. The Young Thing re-enters.*)

YOUNG THING.

Don't the boat feel tilty, or like that?

HUSBAND.

WE ONLY
HAVE A LITTLE TIME.

YOUNG THING.

What?

HUSBAND.

WE ... WE ... WE
HAVE TO SPEND IT WISELY ...

I ... I
WANT TO SPEND MY TIME WITH YOU ...

YOUNG THING.
    Sir ...

HUSBAND.
    LISTEN TO THE MUSIC.
    EVERYTHING IS FINE.
    SO HERE, LET'S HAVE SOME BUBBLY.
    IS THAT YOUR GLASS OR MINE?

YOUNG THING.   *(Suspiciously.)*
    Mine ...

HUSBAND.
    WHILE YOU'RE YOUNG YOU MUSTN'T SQUANDER
    A SPLENDID NIGHT SUCH AS THIS.
    LISTEN TO THE MUSIC
    AND GIVE AN OLD MAN
    A KISS ...

YOUNG THING.
    WHAT'S THE RUSH? — LET'S NOT GO OVERBOARD.
    DON'T FORGET; YOU'RE A GENTLEMAN
    AND I'M — A CATHOLIC.
    TAKE IT SLOW; YOU'VE HAD ALOT OF WINE?
    I SWEAR THE BOAT IS TILTY AND IT'S —

HUSBAND.
    HAVE A CHOC'LATE —
    LISTEN TO THE MUSIC.
    MUSIC DOESN'T LIE.
    IT SAYS I'VE FOUND AN ANGEL
    AND NOW I'D LIKE TO FLY.
(The Prima Donna cries out from the boat deck, struggling with the Steward.)

PRIMA DONNA.

No!!! Don't make me get into the boat! I won't leave my husband!! Nooooo!!!

HUSBAND.

CAN'T YOU HEAR THE CELLO SIGHING?
IN EVERY NOTE LIES A TRUTH:
LISTEN TO THE MUSIC
AND GIVE AN OLD MAN
HIS YOUTH ...

(A flare goes off. An edge of panic underscores The Husband's seduction.)

THIS ALL WILL PASS;
THIS SHIP OF DREAMS.
THIS WORLD WILL DISAPPEAR.
MY LIFE WILL PASS
BUT TILL IT DOES
I'D LIKE TO LIVE WHAT'S LEFT OF IT
RIGHT HERE:
AND DRINK TO US!

(He leaps on a chair.)

AND TOAST TO YOU!
AND TOAST MYSELF!
MYSELF! MYSELF! MYSELF! MYSELF —

YOUNG THING.

Carl ...

(The Young Thing holds out a hand. The Husband takes it. Young Thing leads. The Husband tangos with an angel while all around, the world falls apart. The ship of dreams develops a serious tilt; terrible groans and screams are heard. The Husband collapses into a chair.)

Some party goin' on up there on deck.
... WHEN WE LAND IN NEW YORK
I SUPPOSE WE'LL BE KEEPING IN TOUCH.
RIGHT?
WHEN I LIVE IN NEW YORK
I SUPPOSE YOU WILL ASK ME TO SUP.
SIR?
'COURSE TO LIVE IN NEW YORK
I'LL BE NEEDING SOME HELP SETTING UP ... CARL?

HUSBAND.

The ship has struck an iceberg. We are sinking. Lifeboats are being
lowered. We will die soon.

YOUNG THING.

Oh ... that's good. I never heard that one before.
(A sudden lurch — screams.)
The ship is sinking — and you didn't tell me! You son of a bitch!

HUSBAND.

LISTEN TO THE MUSIC ...
MUSIC DOESN'T LIE ...

YOUNG THING.

Go to hell!!
(The Young Thing grabs the brooch and dashes off.)

HUSBAND.

I THOUGHT I'D FOUND AN ANGEL ...
(He pours himself a glass of champagne and waits. Cacophony.)

SCENE 7

*The screams of drowning passengers segue into the screams of partying discotheque
patrons. The Writer in hip 70s fashion boogies down.*

WRITER.

OPENING MONTAGE:
LIGHTS – TRAFFIC – DOGSHIT – SCREAMS.
MANHATTAN!
WORKING TITLE: "THE ONE I LOVE."
STARRING ME: ME.

SCREENPLAY: ME.

DIRECTED BY: DE PALMA.

NO.

... ME.

LONG SHOT:

THE HOT PLACE.

THE "IN" PLACE.

"THE" PLACE:

TONIGHT.

FRIDAY NIGHT.

MAY THE TWELFTH.

NINETEEN SEVENTY-SIX A.D.

PAN ACROSS THE ROOM — NO:

CLOSE UP: ME.

LOOKING GOOD. LOOKING HOT.

NOW PAN ACROSS THE ROOM:

AND EVERYBODY IS

SMOKING THIS

AND SNORTING THAT

AND LOOKING FOR THIS

AND LOOKING FOR THAT —

AND ZOOM ACROSS THE ROOM:

(The Young Thing appears.)

IT'S AN ANGEL ...

CUT TO:

(He boogies over to the Young Thing.)

Hi.

PRETTY DECENT MUSIC.

YOUNG THING.

It's giving me a headache. I need a drink.

WRITER.

Don't we all need something — anything that will quench our thirst for
Beauty and end our search for happiness?

YOUNG THING.
>A beer's fine.

WRITER.
>Perfection. Oblivious. Perfection.
>CUT TO:
>DANCE FLOOR.

(They dance.)
>... and I write poetry. Mostly free-verse.

YOUNG THING.
>Yeah, well, great ....

WRITER.
>And I dabble in theatre.... And I enjoy writing music.

YOUNG THING.
>Uh-huh.

WRITER.
>I'm all over the place. Artistically. Now I'm working on a screenplay for Newman.

YOUNG THING.
>Paul Newman?

WRITER.
>What's your name?

YOUNG THING.
>Jackie.

WRITER.
>JACKIE THE ANGEL.
>JACKIE MY NEW-FOUND MUSE.

YOUNG THING.
>So you gonna grab us a cab or what?

WRITER.

    CUT TO: LATER. HOME. MINE.

    FUTON – CANDLES – INCENSE – REEFER.

    AND JACKIE THE ANGEL SAYS:

YOUNG THING.

    You made it sound bigger. Where does he sleep?

WRITER.

    Who?

YOUNG THING.

    Paul Newman. You said he stays here when he visits New York.

WRITER.

    Well. Paul's an artist. The couch is just fine by him. Silence: Bergman. Tight shot:

YOUNG THING.

    I'M STONED.

WRITER.

    What do you do, Jackie?

YOUNG THING.

    Temp.

WRITER.

    CLOSEUP: ME.

    What is it you really want to do?

YOUNG THING.

    ...? Temp...?

WRITER.

    I wish I could get inside your little head and see the world as you see it! I want to experience what you experience. But that would probably ruin things, wouldn't it?

YOUNG THING.

    You talk a lot.

WRITER.   *(Pulling the Young Thing to the bed.)*

    Tell me what you desire most —no, let me guess.... No, tell me.... Have you found your ideal lover?

YOUNG THING.

    WHAT'S WITH ALL THE QUESTIONS?

WRITER.

    I want to know every single beautiful thing about you.

YOUNG THING.   *(As they get down to the business of sex.)*

    I SURVIVED A SHIPWRECK.

    THAT WAS SUNDAY NIGHT.

    I SURVIVED A PLANE CRASH.

    THAT WAS MONDAY NIGHT.

    TUESDAY DROPPED SOME ACID.

    THURSDAY WENT TO SLEEP.

    DREAMED THAT I WAS FLOATING FLOATING FLOATING

    IN RICHARD NIXON'S POOL.

    I DON'T KNOW HOW I GET TO

    WHERE I DON'T KNOW WHERE I'M AT.

    BEFORE THERE'S TIME TO THINK

    I EITHER CRASH OR SINK.

    I DON'T KNOW HOW I GET TO

    WHERE I DON'T KNOW WHERE I'M AT.

    THERE'S SOMETHING WRONG WITH THAT.

    THERE'S SOMETHING WRONG WITH THAT.

(The Young Thing steps out of the 'frame.')

    THERE'S SOMETHING WRONG THERE'S SOMETHING WRONG

    THERE'S SOMETHING WRONG

    WHEN ALL I WANT IS

    SOMEWHERE SAFE.

    ANYWHERE, ANYWHERE SAFE.

    WITH SOMEONE WHO WON'T FALL APART

    WHEN THE WORLD BEGINS TO FALL APART.

SOMEONE SINGLE, NOT TOO DULL OR SMART
BUT SAFE;
DECENTLY, HONESTLY SAFE.
WHERE I FIND THAT SOMEONE I DON'T CARE;
JUST AS LONG AS I CAN WIND UP THERE:
SOMEWHERE, SOMEWHERE.
SOMEWHERE SAFE ...

(The Young Thing returns to the action on the futon.)

GOT NO EXPECTATIONS.
USED TO, NOW I DON'T.
I SURVIVED A SHIPWRECK.
I CAN HANDLE IT.
I CAN HANDLE IT.
I CAN HANDLE IT.
I CAN HANDLE —

WRITER/YOUNG THING.

You — You —You —YOU!

(They climax, collapsing into a tangled heap on the futon.)

WRITER.

Done.... Done.... Done ...
CUT TO:
OVERHEAD SHOT.
AFTER.
LOVERS IN BED.
ZEFFIRELLI.
"A TIME FOR US."
MUSIC FROM THE PLACE NEXT DOOR.
SOMETHING SWEET AND FOLKISH.
AND JACKIE THE ANGEL SAYS:

YOUNG THING.

The couch would've been better.

WRITER.

No.
JACKIE THE ANGEL SAYS:

57

YOUNG THING.

    The couch would've been —

WRITER.

    No.

    JACKIE THE ANGEL SAYS:

(The Writer creates a lovely post-coital atmosphere. He imagines the Young Thing saying.)

    THE ONE I LOVE

    KISSES ME

    AND I'M SAFE.

    THE ONE I LOVE

    TOUCHES ME

    AND I FLOAT.

    THE ONE I LOVE IS HERE

    HOLDING ME; FINALLY;

    YOU TOOK SO LONG FOR ME TO FIND.

    THE WORLD CAN END TOMORROW;

    I'VE FOUND THE ONE I LOVE;

    I DON'T MIND.

(The Young Thing falls into the imagined script. They sing together.)

WRITER/YOUNG THING.

    THE ONE I LOVE

    KISSES ME

    AND I'M SAFE.

    THE ONE I LOVE

    TOUCHES ME

    AND I FLOAT.

    THE ONE I LOVE IS HERE

YOUNG THING.

    PART OF ME —

WRITER.

    PART OF ME —

YOUNG THING.

    GIVING ME —

WRITER.
GIVING ME —

WRITER/YOUNG THING.
NEEDING ME NEEDING ME NEEDING ME
MY LOVER KISSES ME GOOD NIGHT.
THE WORLD CAN END TOMORROW
THE ONE I LOVE AND I;
WE'LL SLEEP TIGHT …

WRITER.
BUT. CUT.
NOBODY SAYS THAT.
JACKIE THE ANGEL SAYS:

YOUNG THING.
THE ONE I LOVE KISSES —

WRITER.
No.
JACKIE THE ANGEL SAYS:

YOUNG THING.
… the couch would've been better. How long you had this mattress?

WRITER.
Futon. Ah well…. Are you hungry?

YOUNG THING.
Can I read your screenplay?

WRITER.
Read?

YOUNG THING.
I heard alot of stories. I could tell you if yours was any good.

WRITER.

It's not finished. But food always leads to inspiration. There's a deli on the corner, let's —

YOUNG THING.

THIS IS OKAY.

I DON'T MIND YOUR FUTON.

WRITER.

How lovely that word sounds coming from you

"FUTON."

Where are my shoes?

CUT TO:

(He exits.)

YOUNG THING.

WHY BOTHER?

CREDITS.

FADE OUT.

ONCE AGAIN.

THE END.

SCENE 8

A silent movie. 1920s. The Writer narrates.

WRITER.   *(Voice-over.)*

All right everybody, let's take this again.

"THE ONE I LOVE"

Directed by Me. Written by Me. Starring Me ... and She. Take twelve.

The Playwright attempts to seduce his Leading Lady during a romantic weekend tryst at the Spa.

(The Writer and the Actress arrive at the spa; chaise, dressing screen. The Writer carries several suitcases. They pantomime the dialogue, which appears as surtitles — or with the continued voice-over of the Writer who speaks both parts.)

ACTRESS.

"Where have you taken me, scoundrel?"

WRITER.

"You suggested the Spa, Angel."

ACTRESS.

"How nice it is to take a respite from the stage."
(She flings open a window. Moonlight streams in.)
"Ah! The moonlight!"
(Moved. She kneels and prays. The Writer kneels beside her and caresses her.)

WRITER.

"To whom are you praying?"

ACTRESS.

"To you, my creator!"

WRITER.

"Kiss me."

ACTRESS.

"Now I must prepare my toilette!"
(She goes behind the screen and disrobes.)

WRITER.

("I must entice her to do my new play.") "You are the vessel into which
I pour my soul! Let us consummate our love; Artist and Muse!"

ACTRESS.

"Come and tell me the plot of your new play."
*(She re-emerges from behind the screen and stretches out on the chaise. He joins her and
describes his newest masterpiece and the magnificent role he has written for her.)*

WRITER.

"I have written you the role of a lifetime!"   "An innocent, helpless waif."

ACTRESS.

"But I must play a sensual creature — a modern woman! I cannot play a lie!"

WRITER.

"You shall play the part I wrote for you."
(Which is an innocent, helpless waif. She won't stand for it. They argue violently. The fight turns to passion. She is in control. The Writer cries "Cut," but to no avail. She devours him. A pause. Exhausted, he speaks aloud, onstage.)

Cut. Cut.

ACTRESS.   *(Continuing to pantomime her lines, which continue as subtitles or voice-over.)*

"What a wonderful idea it was to come to the spa."

WRITER.

Say that you love me.

ACTRESS.

"I shall breathe fire into my new role!"

WRITER.

Say that you love me. Say the words.

ACTRESS.

"I do inspire you, don't I?"
(Happily, she skips off to the mudbaths.)

WRITER.

Say that you ... you ...

CREDITS.

FADE OUT.

ONCE AGAIN.

THE END.

(A slow pin-spot fades à la Charlie Chaplin.)

SCENE 9

1980s. The Company, save The Whore, watches music videos, using remotes to switch channels.

VIDEO ONE. *(Soldier.)*

> CHUCK 'N DI 'N BURT 'N LONI
> NANCY RON, 'N ED 'N JOHNNY
> LET'S GO SPEEDIN' THROUGH THE EIGHTIES
> SLEEP IT OFF AT WARREN BEATTY'S
> EVERYBODY ROCK.
> ROCK WITH ROCK WITH ROCK WITH ROCK WITH

VIDEO TWO. *(Nurse.)*

> I WANNA BE YOUR ANGEL OF MERCY
> I WANNA BE YOUR VERY FIRST TIME.
> I WANNA BE YOUR FAVORITE LOVE TOY.
> I WANNA BE YOUR ANGEL TONIGHT —

(Company switches on the Actress' terrace. City skyline. Evening. The Actress and the Senator enter.)

ACTRESS.

> You're not going anywhere — See? I arranged for this beautiful view —

SENATOR.

> Sally ...

ACTRESS.

> My Senator doesn't visit New York as much as he used to.

SENATOR.

> You know I've been busy.

ACTRESS.

> My Senator doesn't call half as often as he used to. Are you cheating on me?

SENATOR.

No ... Sally.... Dinner was terrific, but —
I'D BETTER SAY GOODNIGHT.

ACTRESS.

WHY?

SENATOR.

I've got an early morning breakfast. The Mayor.

ACTRESS.

THEN IT'S SHUTTLE BACK TO LITTLE WASHINGTON
LEAVING ME ALONE ON MY BIG OLD PATIO
WITH NOTHING TO DO.

SENATOR.

You're shooting a new movie, right? "The role of a lifetime," you said.

ACTRESS.

IT'S KILLING ME.
I'M DYING.
SEE?
I'M ALMOST DEAD.

SENATOR.

It's funny. I remember you saying "I'm an artist — I only do what's good
for my soul."

ACTRESS.

I'd be happier doing something else.

SENATOR.

Happiness doesn't exist.
IT'S A LIE.

ACTRESS.

Oh?

SENATOR.

Yes. The Constitution guarantees people the right to spend their whole lives pursuing … A LIE.

ACTRESS.

A LIE.

SENATOR.

BUT —

ACTRESS.

BUT?

SENATOR.

OTHER THINGS.

ACTRESS.

LIKE?

SENATOR.

LIKE …

ACTRESS.

PLEASURE.

SENATOR.

PLEASURE IS REAL.

ACTRESS.

REAL!

SENATOR.

And good wine and good food and good company and once a week … a good movie. Starring you.
I LIKE TO KNOW WHEN I'M ENJOYING MYSELF
WHENEVER I'M ENJOYING MYSELF.

ACTRESS.

    ... ENJOY!

SENATOR.

    WE MAY DIE TOMORROW.

ACTRESS.

    CANCELLED!

SENATOR.

    Right!
    "WHAT WOULD HAVE BEEN" IS SAD.
    "LATER ON" IS ...

ACTRESS.

    SAD!

SENATOR.

    SAD.

ACTRESS.

    MY CONGRESSMAN THE PHILOSOPHER.

SENATOR.

    YOUR CONGRESSMAN SHOULD SAY GOODNIGHT.

ACTRESS.

    Stop ... this. You're teasing me. I've been waiting to see you all week.

SENATOR.

    We'll have dinner tomorrow.

ACTRESS.

    A lot of other men would be more then happy to be right here, right *now* alone with me.

SENATOR.

    Well. I'm happy ...

ACTRESS.

Uh-oh! You said happiness was a lie.... Did I say something to scare you?

SENATOR.

Sally, this arrangement we have ... it's —

ACTRESS.

Real.

SENATOR.

— we shouldn't pretend —

ACTRESS.

Stop.

SENATOR.

— the truth is —

ACTRESS.

Shh.

I CAN PLAY THE MISTRESS OF THE SENATOR.

STASH ME IN A COMFORTABLE HIGH-RISE

THAT'S CONVENIENT TO THE HILL.

AND AFTER MAKING SOME SPEECH

OR SIGNING SOME BILL

YOU'LL DROP IN FOR LUNCH

AND IF YOU NEVER TAKE LUNCH

WITH ME AROUND, YOU WILL.

I'LL PLAY THE MISTRESS OF THE SENATOR.

I LOOK GOOD IN RED OR WHITE OR BLUE.

I'LL BE FRIENDLY TO REPUBLICANS.

I'LL BE ANYTHING FOR YOU.

SENATOR.

You don't have to "be" anything for me, Sally ...

I HAVE TO SAY GOODNIGHT.

(She won't let him get away. He's not playing his part the way he's expected to.)

ACTRESS.

      I CAN PLAY ADVISOR TO THE CONGRESSMAN
      HIRE ME TO WORK ON YOUR IMAGE.
      I'LL MANIPULATE THE PRESS.
      WE'LL BUY A REGISTERED HOUSE WITH A
      GEORGETOWN ADDRESS, WE'LL WRITE THE PLACE OFF
      AS A WORK EXPENSE AND SCREW THE I.R.S.
      I'LL PLAY ADVISOR TO THE CONGRESSMAN.
      THAT'S A ROLE THAT TAKES ALOT OF SOUL
      TO DO.
      I'LL BE USEFUL DOWN IN WASHINGTON.
      I'LL BE ANYTHING FOR YOU.
      I NEED A CHANGE OF SCENERY.
      I NEED A NEW CAREER.
      I NEED A NEW ADVENTURE, AND
      I CAN'T WAIT ANOTHER YEAR.
      I CAN'T WAIT ANOTHER DAY,
      NOT WHEN I HAVE YOU.
      YOU NEED TO WIN IMPORTANT RACES.
      I NEED TO PLAY IN BETTER PLACES.
      LET ME PLAY THE LOVER OF THE PRESIDENT;
      SET UP IN A WING OF THE WHITE HOUSE,
      WE CAN SHARE THE SWIMMING POOL.
      YOU'LL LET ME DECIDE WHO'S HOT OR COOL;
      IMPORTANT OR NOT; FRIEND OR FOOL.
      I'LL PLAY LADY BIRD; ROSELYN; PAT.
      I'LL PLAY JACKIE BETTER THAN JACKIE DID
      AND NOT USE A HAT.
      I'LL PLAY THE GOOD WIFE; THE MARTYR;
      THE ASSET; THE PLUS.
      I'LL PLAY MYSELF
      IN THE MOVIE OF US IN THE MOVIE OF US
      IN THE MOVIE OF US IN THE MOVIE OF US —
      YOU NEED A LOVER;
      I'LL BE YOUR LOVER;
      I'LL STAY YOUR LOVER;
      I'LL BE. I'LL BE —
      I'LL BE HAPPY DOWN IN WASHINGTON;

I'LL BE WHAT YOU WANT
I'LL BE ANYTHING
FOR YOU
YOU ... YOU ... YOU. .. YOU
(She devours him. The Company watches. They climax as one.)

Here. I want to give you a present.
(She removes a glittering brooch from her dress.)

SENATOR.

What's this?

ACTRESS.

Diamonds from an admirer.

SENATOR.

I don't want —
(She pins the brooch on his lapel.)

ACTRESS.

Now what do you say?

SENATOR.

Thank you ...

ACTRESS.

No ... what do you say?
(The Senator rises, puts on his coat.)

SENATOR.

I have to go.

ACTRESS.

Go? Yes. You have to go. I must ask you to go. I have to have my rest for tomorrow's shoot; my director will kill me if I oversleep —

SENATOR.

I promise to call when I'm in New York next week.

ACTRESS.

Next week?

SENATOR.

The fund-raiser.

ACTRESS.

But what about tomorrow night?

SENATOR.

Sally. I can't —

ACTRESS.

Eight o-clock would be perfect.

SENATOR.

But it wouldn't be ... I mean — for the soul, this isn't —

ACTRESS.   *(Cutting him off.)*

We're not talking about souls, we're talking about dinner. Have your sec-
retary make reservations at Café des Artistes — it's around the corner
from my studio.

SENATOR.

But — goodnight. *(He exits.)*

ACTRESS.

Sweet dreams, my Congressman! Philosopher! Au revoir!

AU REVOIR ... LITTLE WASHINGTON ...

(She is left alone on the terrace. The Company clicks their remotes off.)

SCENE 10

The Present. A phone is buzzing. The Whore answers. The Senator is calling. (In the New York production, the actors were staged on a simple iron bed. During the phone conversation, they were isolated by light.)

WHORE.
> Hello, this is Lisa.

SENATOR.
> It's me.

WHORE.
> Oh ... hello again. "Senator."

SENATOR.
> I wanted to talk some more ...

WHORE.
> Talk all you like baby.

SENATOR.   *(After a beat.)*
> Is your name really "Lisa?"

WHORE.
> What's wrong with Lisa? Are you really a "Senator?"

SENATOR.
> I guess you're right.

WHORE.
> — HEY IT DON'T MATTER. It's kinky.

SENATOR.
> Am I the only one who calls just to talk?

WHORE.

Nah.... Lots of other do. Some just make noises. It's okay.

SENATOR.

Why do you do what it is you do?

WHORE.

Why do you call?

SENATOR.

I was with someone last night, in a dream.

WHORE.

Mmm ... a fantasy.

SENATOR.

I don't know what it was ... I was ... I don't know where exactly. I woke up in stranger's room. Dark ... almost morning ... almost ...

THE BED WAS NOT MY OWN.
SOMEONE SLEPT WITH ME.
SOMEONE SLEPT BESIDE ME IN THE DARK.
A GIRLFRIEND I KNEW.
MY WIFE AND MY EX —
MY COUSIN MARIE.
THE THING IN THE PARK.
THE BLOND FROM THE BAR.
THE GUY FROM THE GYM.
NOT REALLY HER.
NOT REALLY HIM ...

THE BED WAS NOT MY OWN.
SOMEONE LAY THERE STILL.
SOMEONE WHO WOULD KNOW MY NAME.
WHAT I HOPED TO FIND
IN ALL MY LOVERS —
(WERE THEY LOVERS?)
(CAN I CALL THEM LOVERS?)

WHAT I'D NEVER FOUND
IN ANY LOVER
WAS THERE —
HERE —
SHALLOW BREATH.
SLEEP AND DEATH.
ALL IN ONE.
THE ONLY ONE.

MY DREAM WAS NOT MY OWN.
SOMEONE DREAMED WITH ME.
SOMEONE DREAMED BESIDE ME IN THE DARK.

SLEEP, ANGEL, DON'T WAKE UP.
I AM IN YOUR DREAM.
SLEEP, LOVER, DON'T WAKE UP
OR ELSE OUR DREAM IS DONE ...

DON'T WAKE UP
OR I'LL WAKE UP ALONE
A GIRLFRIEND I KNEW
MY WIFE AND MY EX.
YOU. YOU.

(He is in the Whore's garret. The Whore is fast asleep in bed. The Whore stirs.)

WHORE.

Who...? Oh! Hey handsome ...

SENATOR.

Good morning. I think.

WHORE.

Good morning ...

SENATOR.

Who are you?

WHORE.

Leocadia …

SENATOR.

Leocadia.... You're … beautiful …

WHORE.

Thank you.

SENATOR.

Well.... Good-bye.

WHORE.

Good-bye.

SENATOR.

Should we shake hands or something?

WHORE.

Sure.

SENATOR.

I don't know how I got here …

WHORE.

I usually work the river. Sometimes if I like a guy I bring him back here. All of Marianne's girls work here. Listen — you can hear Emily snoring next door.

SENATOR.

Then I should … pay you.

WHORE.

WHO MENTIONED MONEY?
WHO MENTIONED PAY?

SENATOR.

You don't want anything from me?

74

WHORE;

No handsome. I don't need nothing.

SENATOR.

Leocadia ... last night ... did we.... Were we lovers?

WHORE.

Don't you remember handsome?
(She smiles; she turns away from him.)

SENATOR.

Leocadia? Leocadia ...
(He slips the brooch the Actress gave him under her pillow.)

If I'd only kissed you.

SLEEP ANGEL. DON'T WAKE UP.

I AM IN YOUR DREAM.

SLEEP LOVER, DON'T WAKE UP.

OR ELSE OUR DREAM IS ...
(He picks up his coat, begins to exit.)

WHORE.

HEY THERE.

WHERE YOU GOIN' LOVER?
(Senator stops.)

COME CLOSE.

LET ME SEE YOUR FACE ...
(He goes to her. The Whore kisses him on the lips — It's the first kiss we've seen all evening.)

YOU DON'T HAVE TO REMEMBER

A FACE OR PLACE OR WHEN.

COME FIND ME TOMORROW.

YOU KNOW MY NAME, LOVE.

I'M SURE WE'LL BE SAYING

HELLO ...
(The Senator starts to exit again. One by one, the characters appear.)

SOLDIER.

HELLO AGAIN.

NURSE.

    HELLO AGAIN.

COLLEGE BOY.

    HELLO AGAIN.

YOUNG WIFE.

    HELLO AGAIN.

HUSBAND.

    HELLO AGAIN.

YOUNG THING.

    HELLO AGAIN.

WRITER.

    HELLO AGAIN.

ACTRESS.

    HELLO AGAIN.

ALL.

    HELLO ...

(Before The Senator exits, he turns back to The Whore. The moment is suspended in expectancy. Slow fade.)

The End

PROPERTY LIST

Glass of water (NURSE)
Shoes (YOUNG WIFE)
Gift box with brooch (YOUNG THING)
Brooch (WHORE, YOUNG THING, ACTRESS, SENATOR)
Champagne bottle (HUSBAND)
Champagne glass (HUSBAND)
Suitcases (WRITER)

SOUND EFFECTS

Thunder rolls, distant then approaching
Groans and screams from sinking ship
Screams of partying at discotheque

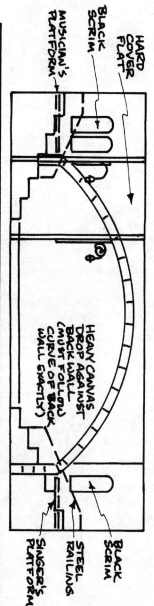

SCENE DESIGN
"HELLO
AGAIN"
(DESIGNED BY
DEREK McLANE
FOR LINCOLN
CENTER THEATER)

FRONT
ELEVATION

HARD
COVER
FLAT

BLACK
SCRIM

MUSICIAN'S
PLATFORM

HEAVY CANVAS
DROP AGAINST
BACK WALL
(MUST FOLLOW
CURVE OF BACK
WALL EXACTLY)

BLACK
SCRIM

STEEL
RAILING

SINGER'S
PLATFORM

MUSICIAN
PLATFORM
(ABOVE)

LAMP POST ON
TRAVEL TRACK

PAINTED CANVAS DROP
WITH BASEBOARD PULLED TIGHT
TO WALL

FIR FLOORING -
DISTRESSED
SANDED & STAINED

BLACK SCRIM

ROLL
DROP

SINGER
PLATFORM
(ABOVE)